KINDERGARTEN LETTER SOUNDS

Fun-filled Activities

An imprint of Om Books International

Beginning a

Read aloud the name of each picture that begins with a.

Draw lines from the pictures the names of which begin with a to the letter a.

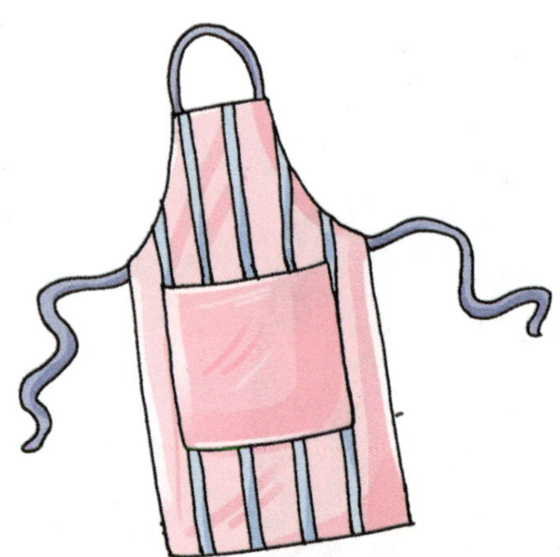

Beginning b

Beginning b sound
bread

Circle (O) the pictures whose names begin with the letter b.

Ending b

Ending b sound
tub

Write b to finish the words that end with b.

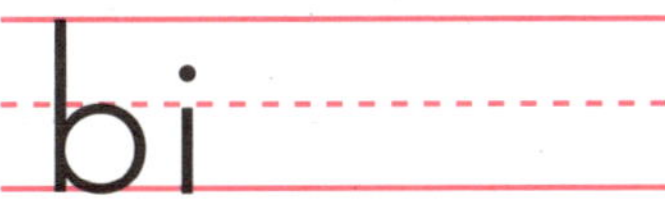

com

thum

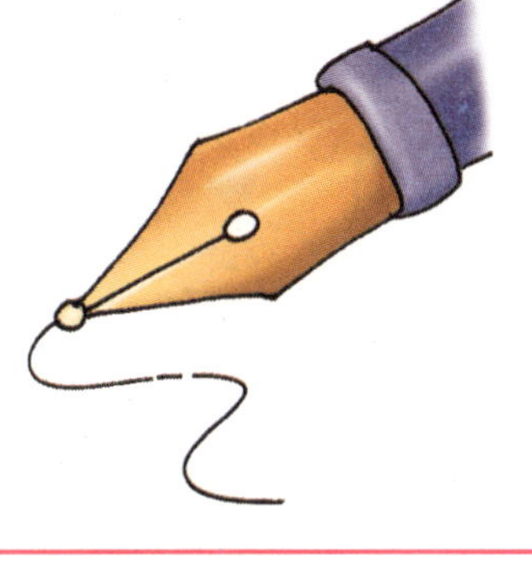

ni

Beginning c

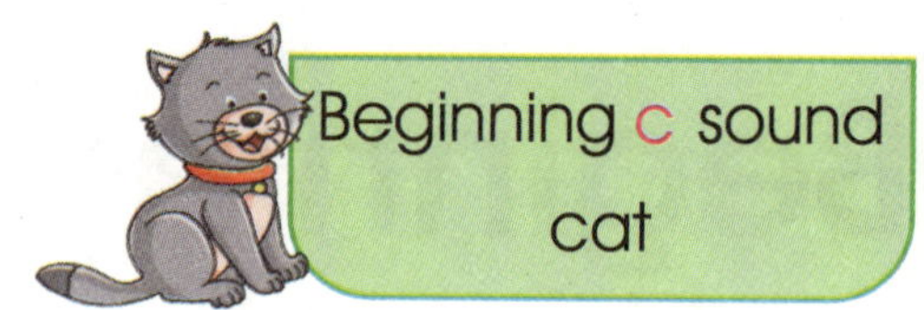

Look at the picture clues.

Write letters to finish each word in the puzzle that begins with c.

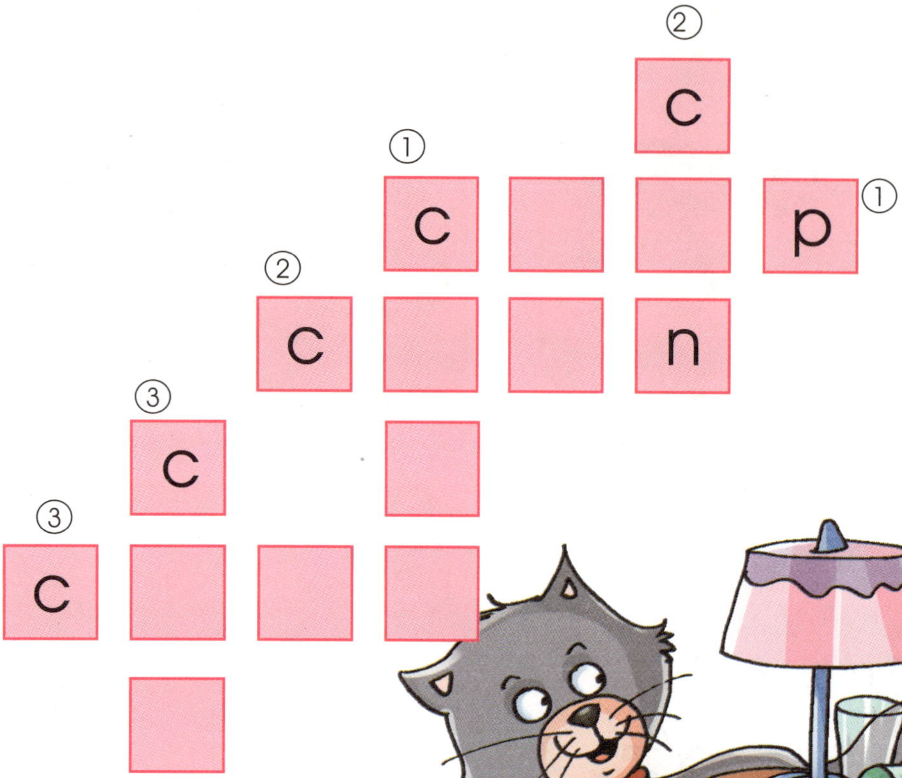

					② c		
			① c			p ①	
		② c			n		
	③ c						
③ c							

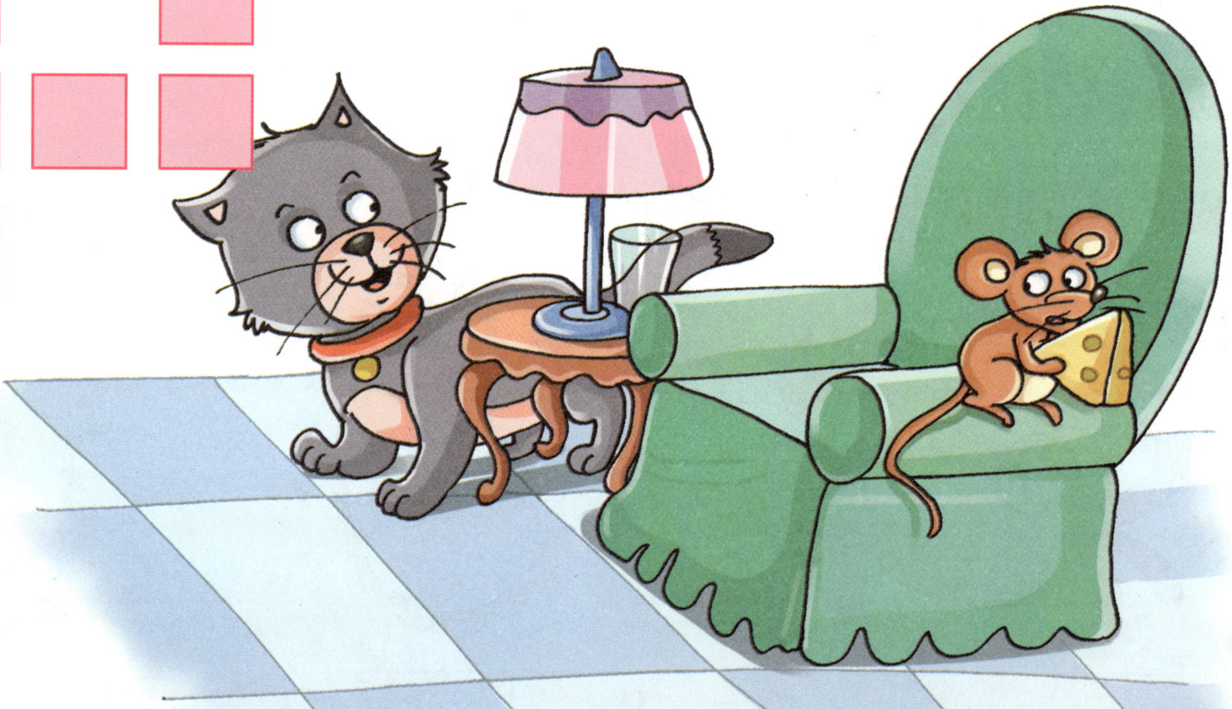

Across

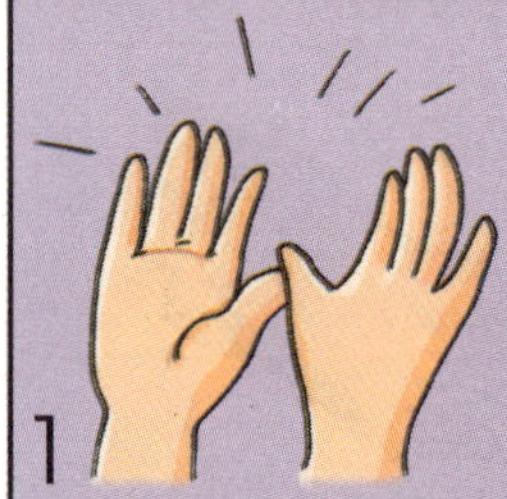

1

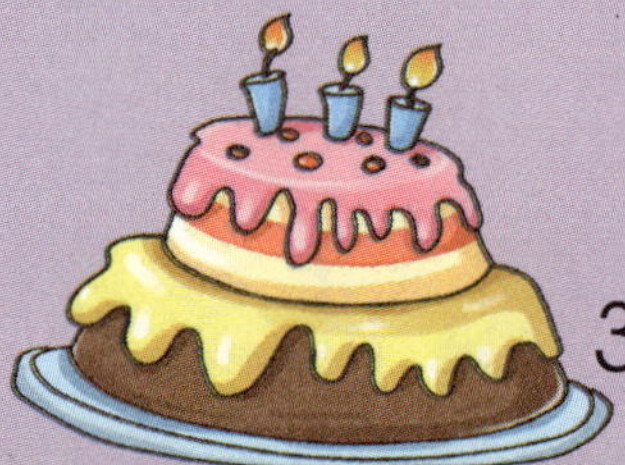

3

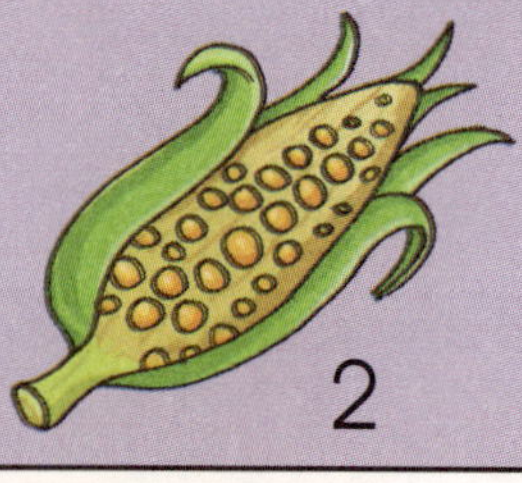

2

Down

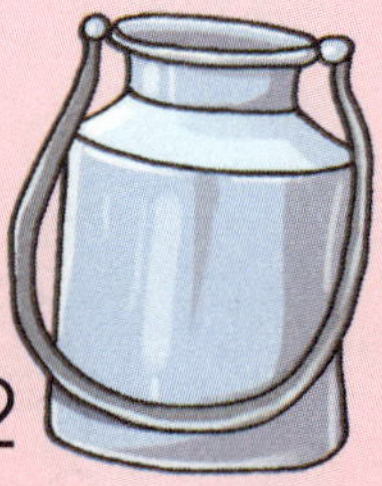

2

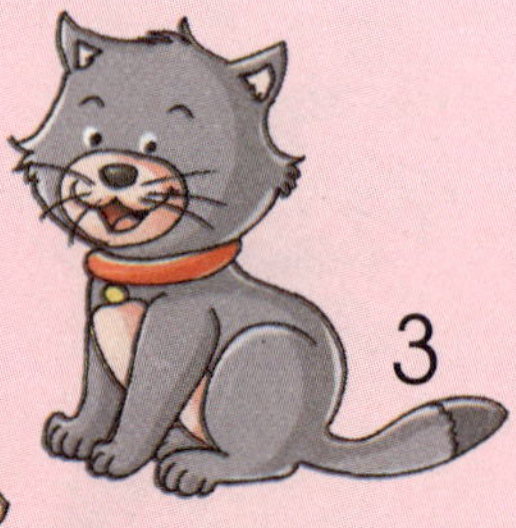

3

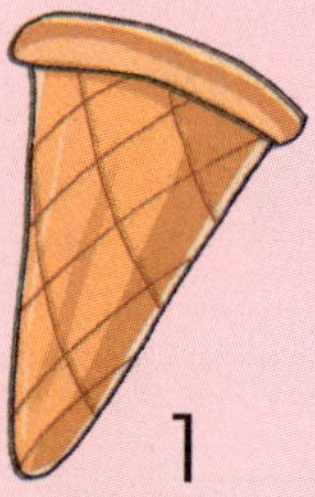

1

Beginning d

Write d under the pictures whose names begin with d.

Ending d

Draw a line through the words that end with letter d.

hand dog robe

seed sand daisy

fish food gold

Beginning e

Beginning e sound
egg

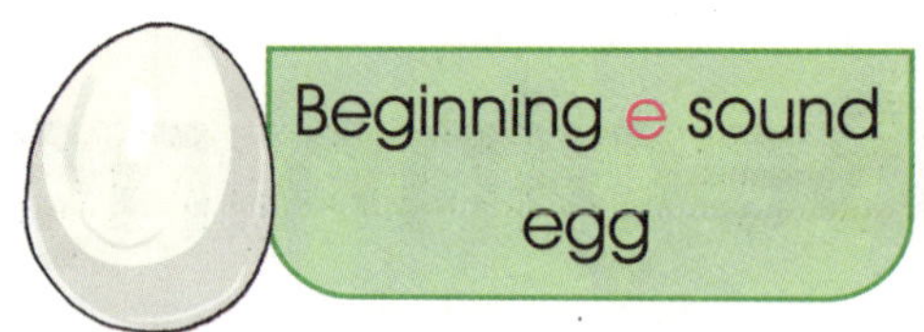

Draw a line from the elephant to each picture whose name begins with e.

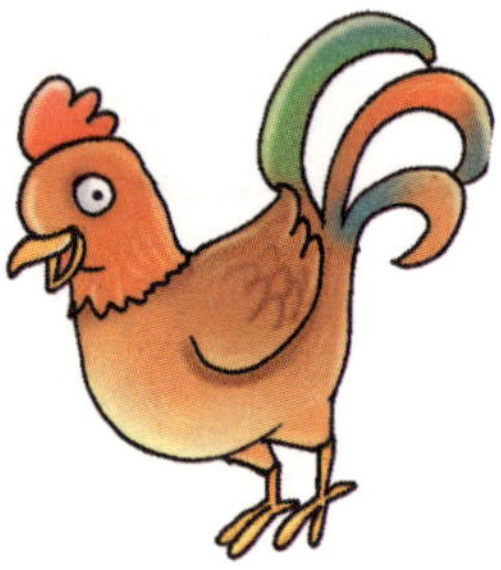

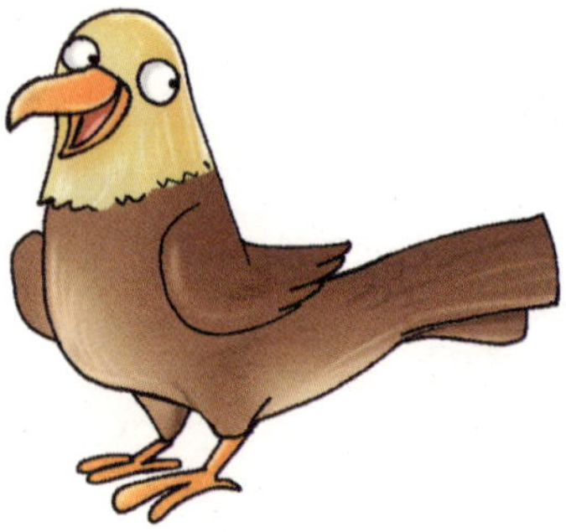

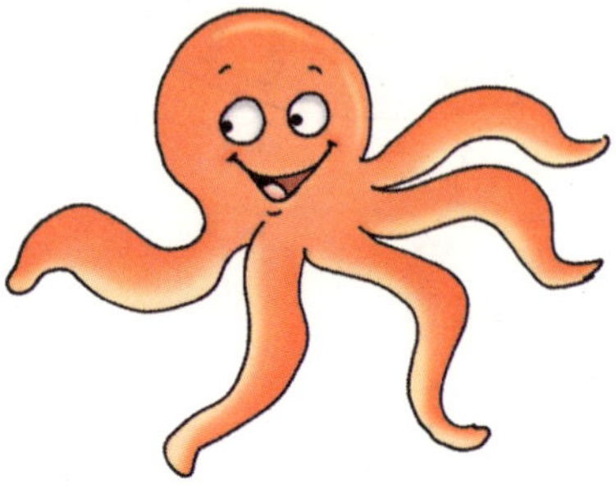

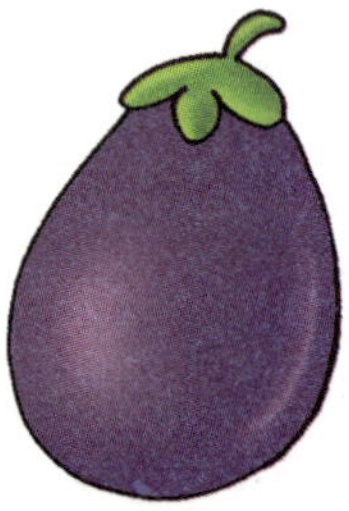

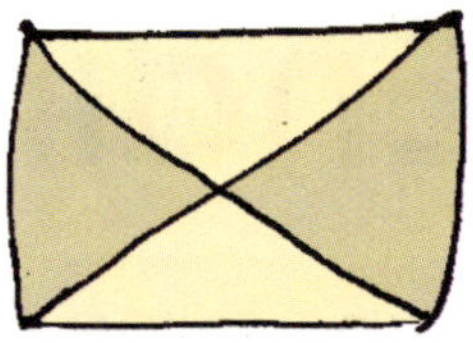

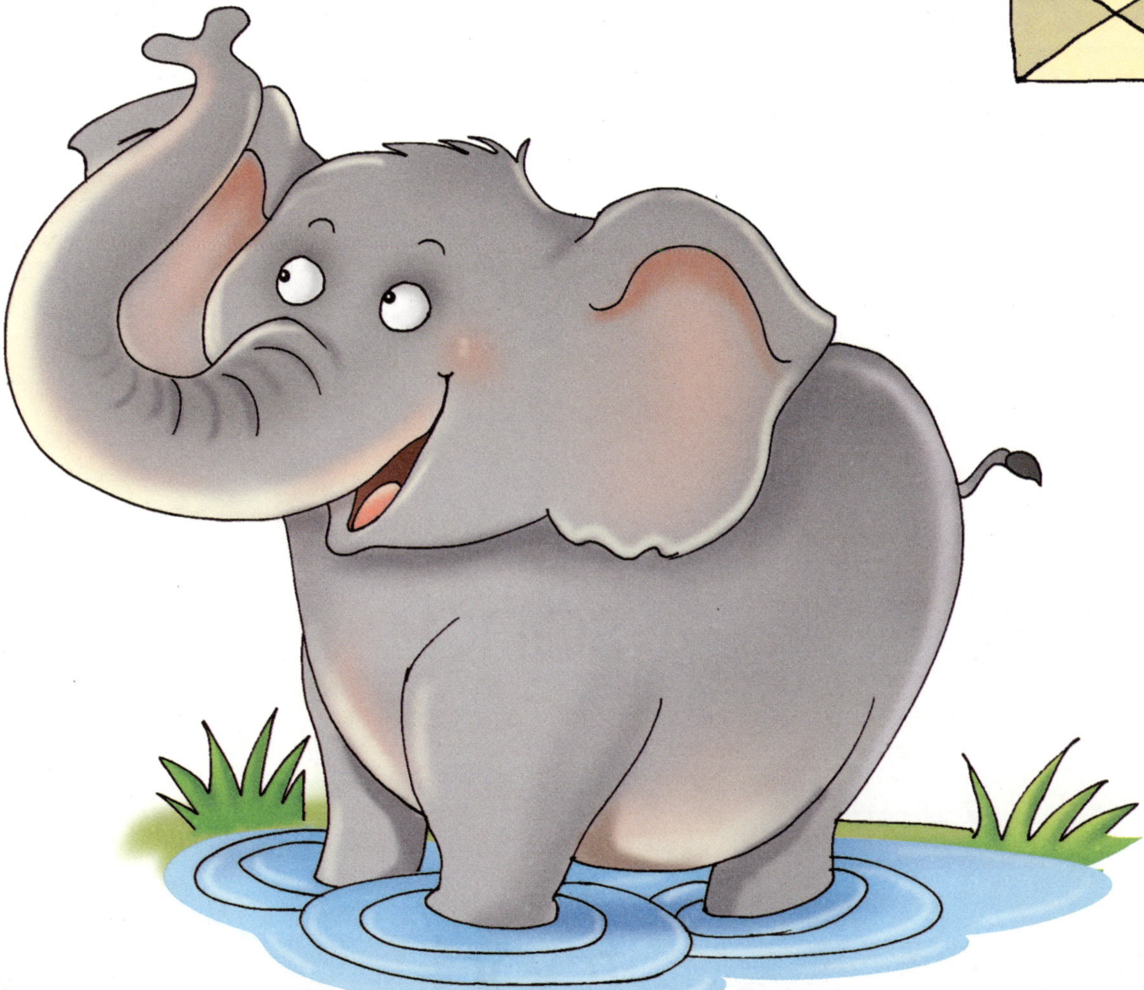

Beginning f

Draw a line from f to each picture whose name begins with f.

f

Ending f

Write f and complete the words that end in f.

loa

che

roo

Beginning g

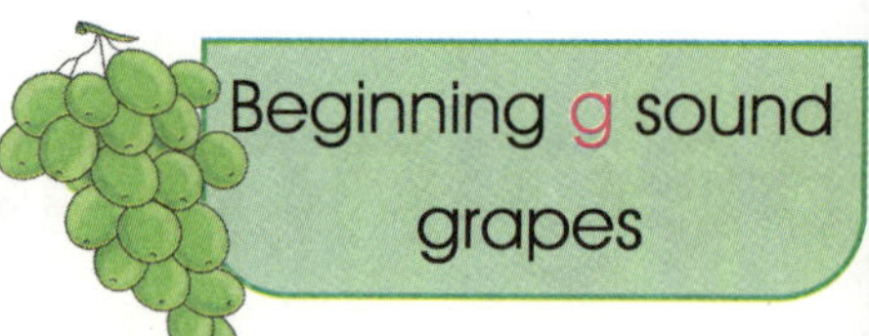

Circle (O) the pictures whose names begin with the letter g.

Ending g

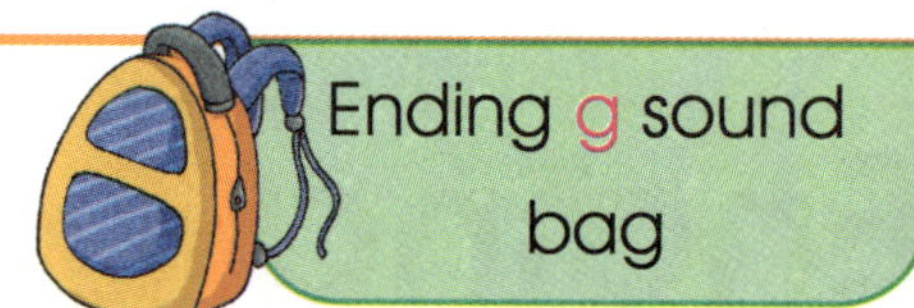

Match the words to the pictures whose names end with letter g.

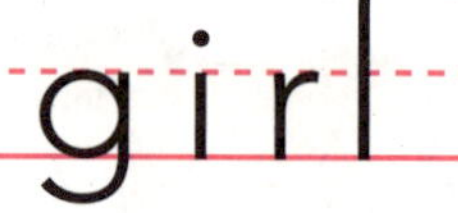

Beginning h

Beginning h sound
horse

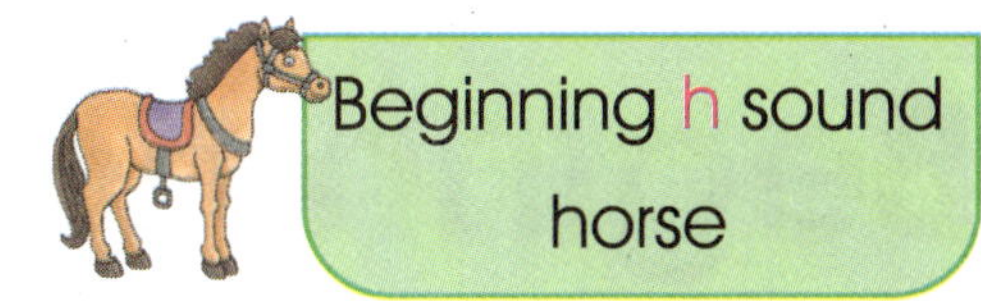

Circle (O) the pictures whose names begin with the letter h.

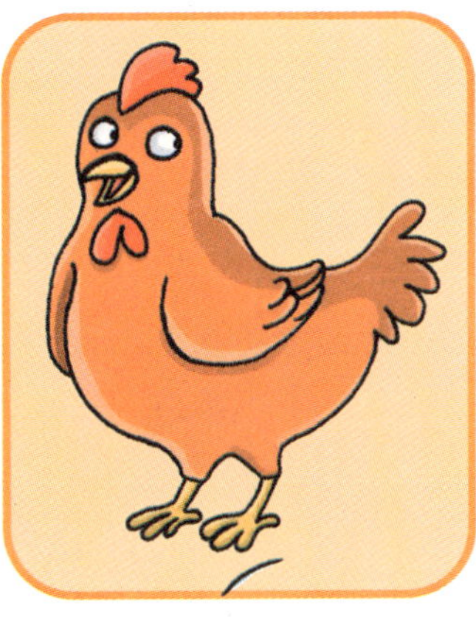

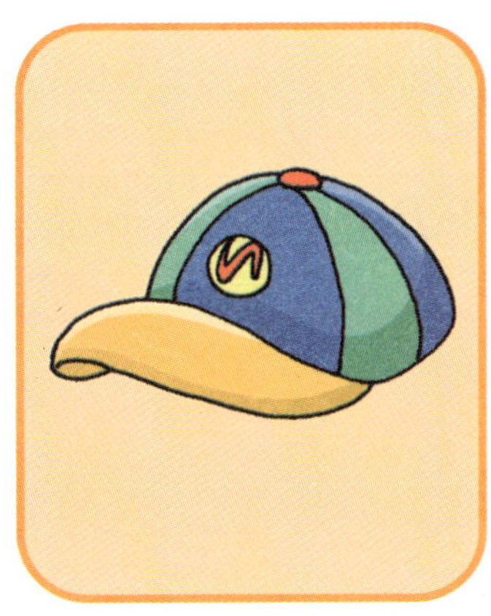

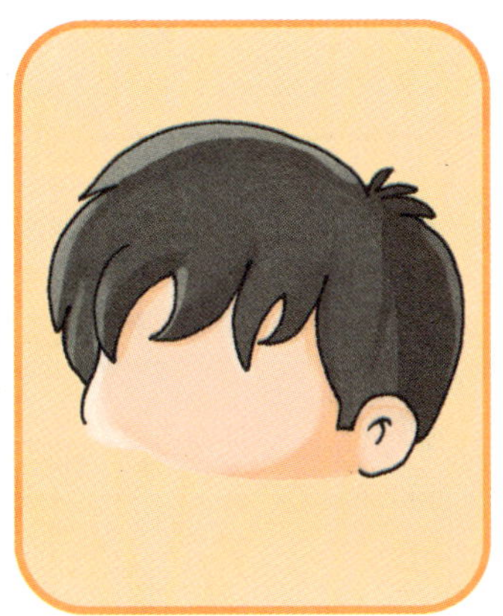

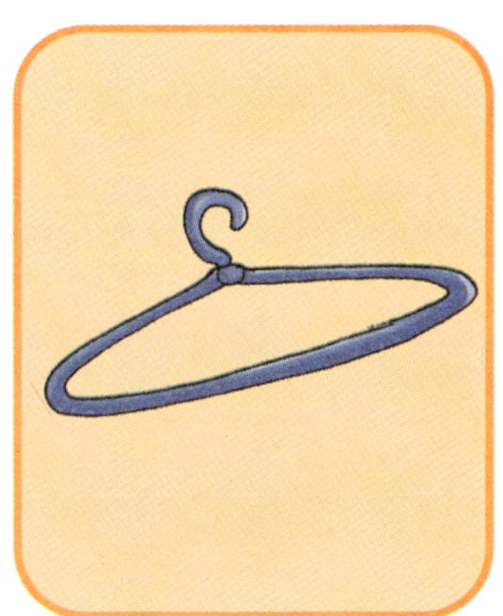

Write h for the pictures whose names start with the same sound as hat.

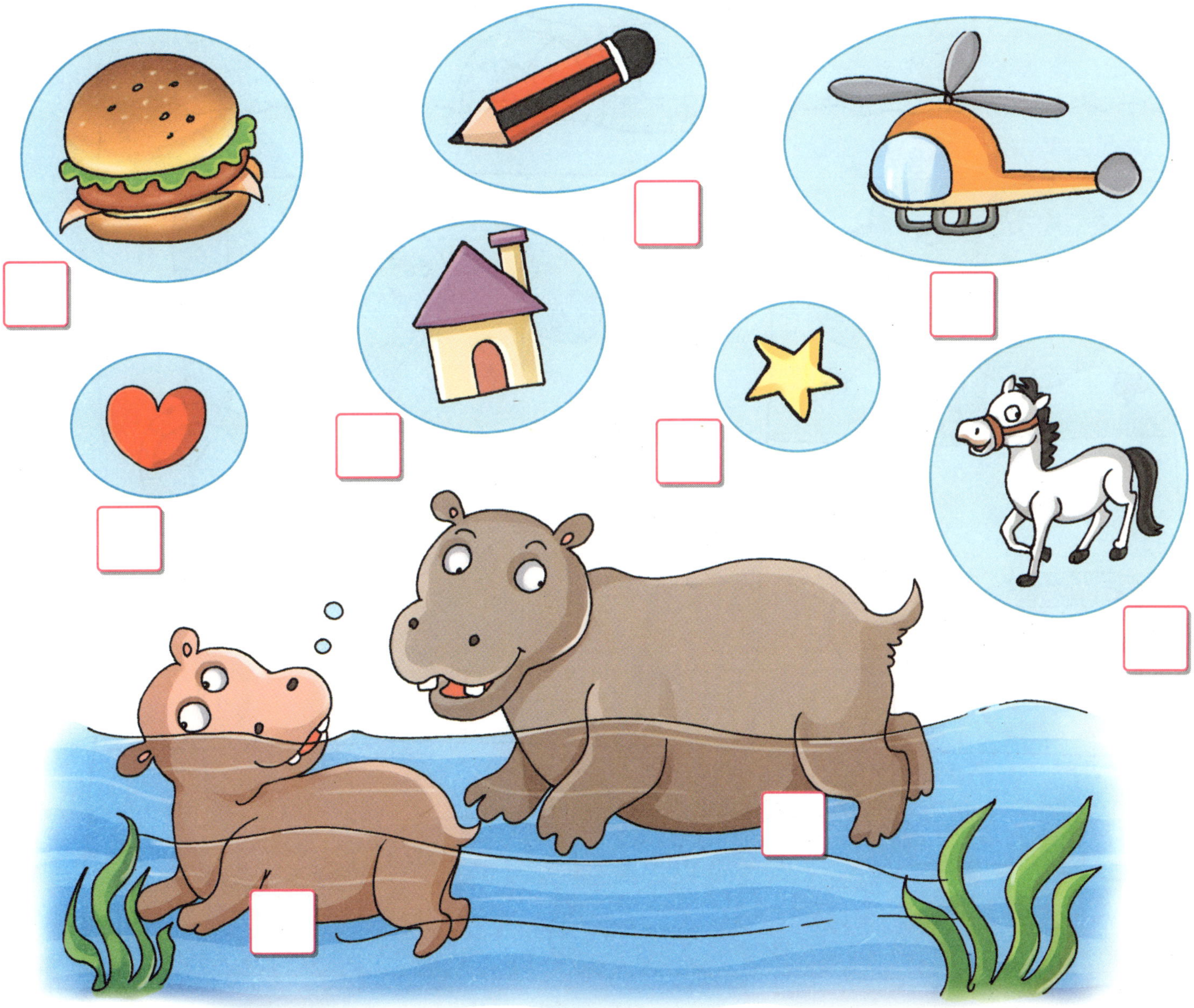

Beginning i

Write i for pictures whose names begin with letter i.

Put a cross (×) on the pictures whose names do not begin with letter i.

Beginning j

Beginning j sound
joker

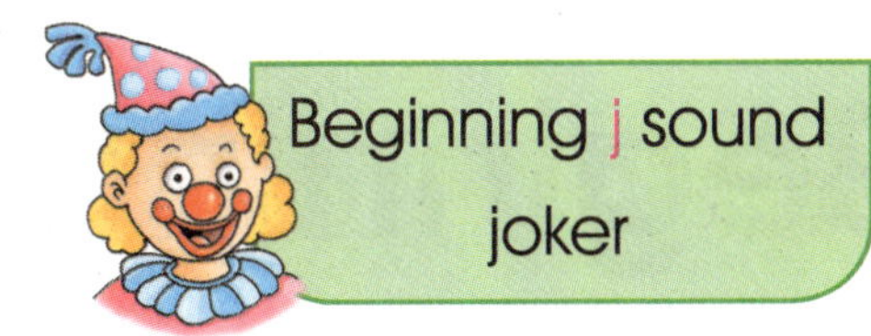

Write j under the pictures whose names begin with j.

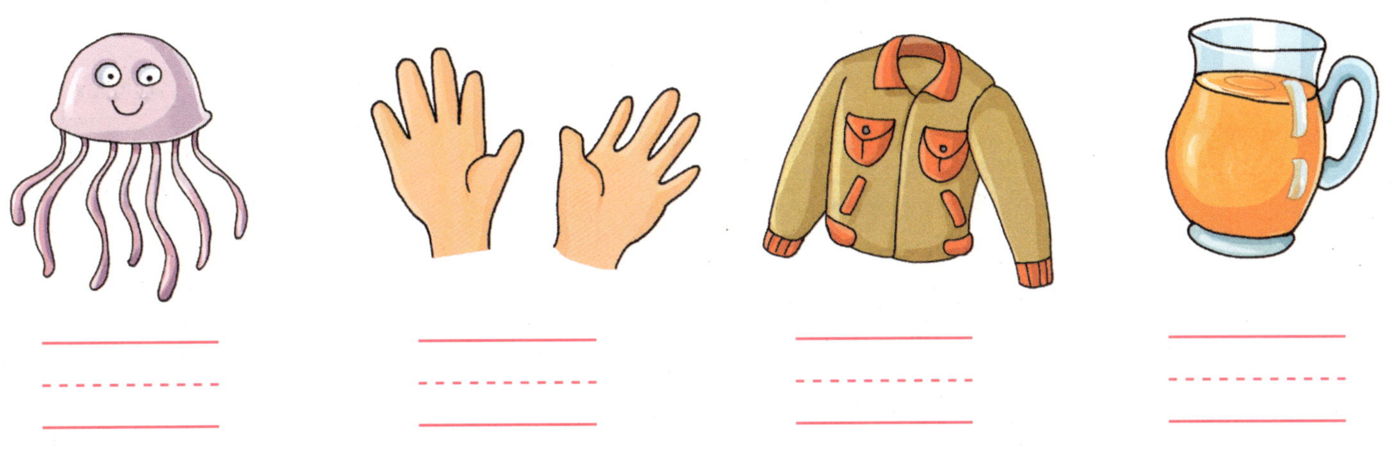

Draw lines from the pictures whose names begin with j to the letter j.

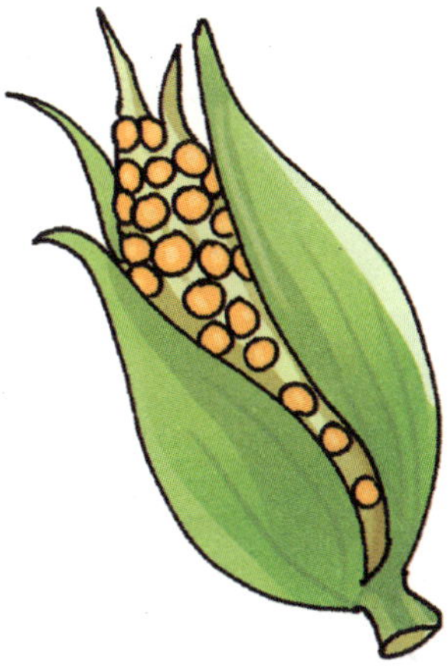

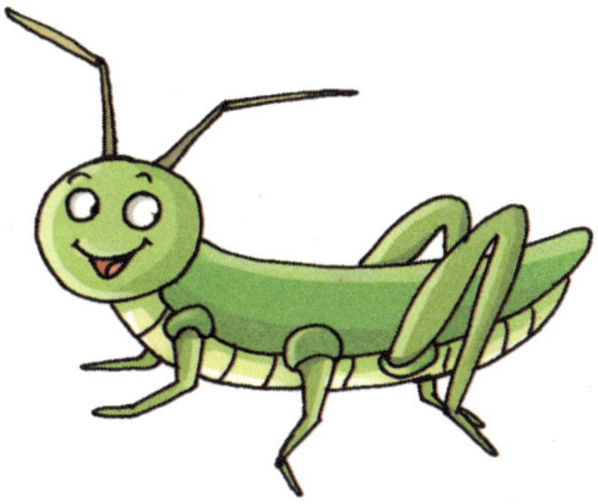

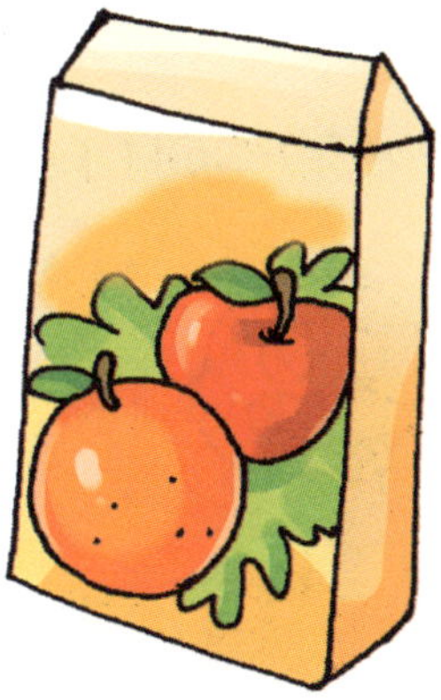

j

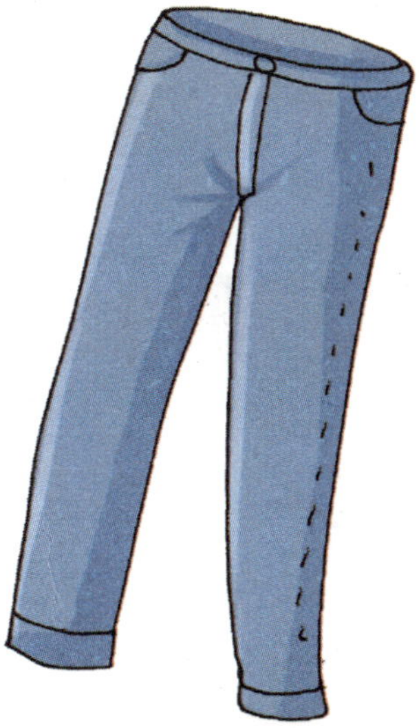

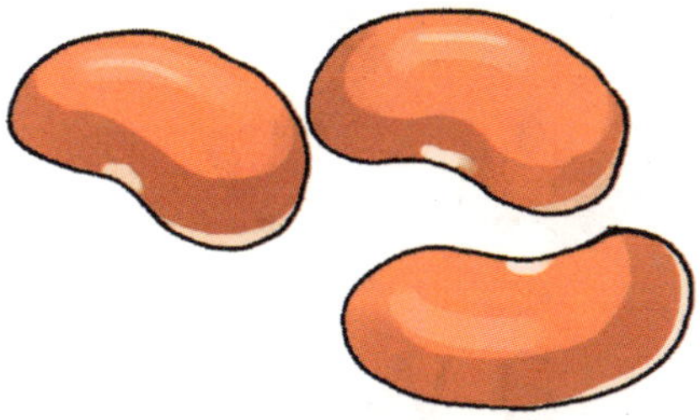

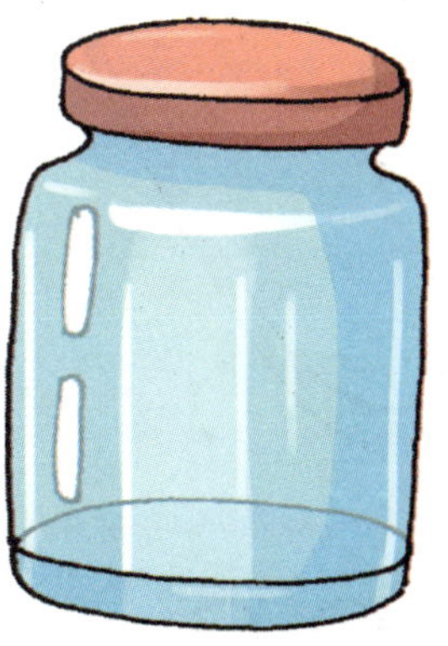

Beginning k

Circle (O) the pictures the names of which begin with k.

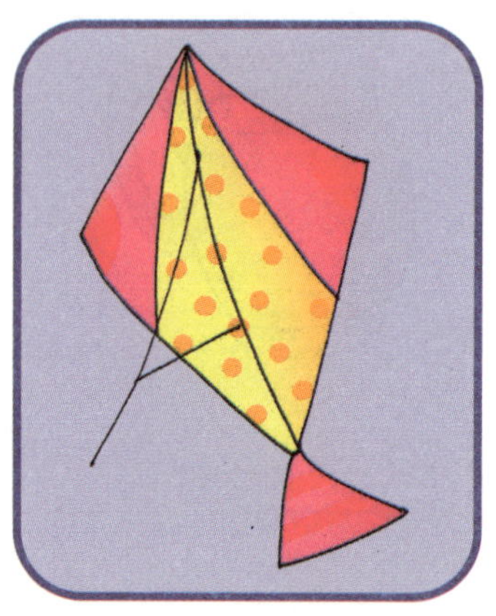

Ending k

Ending k sound
rock

Write k to complete the words that end in k.

duc

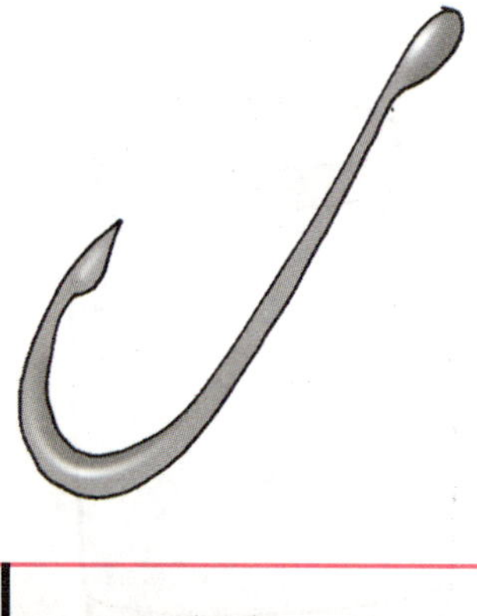

hoo

haw

coc

Beginning l

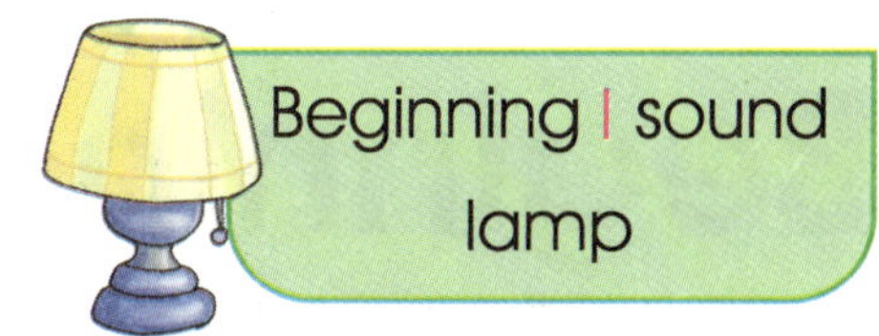

Write l for each picture whose name begins with l.

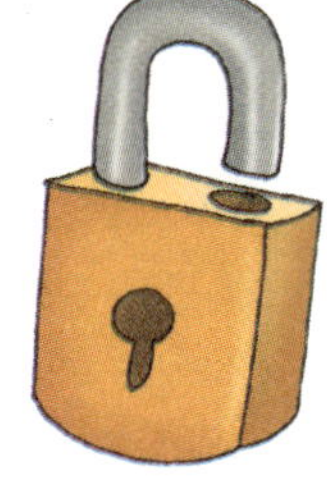

Ending l

Read aloud the name of each picture. Circle (O) the picture whose name ends with l.

Beginning m

Beginning m sound
mouse

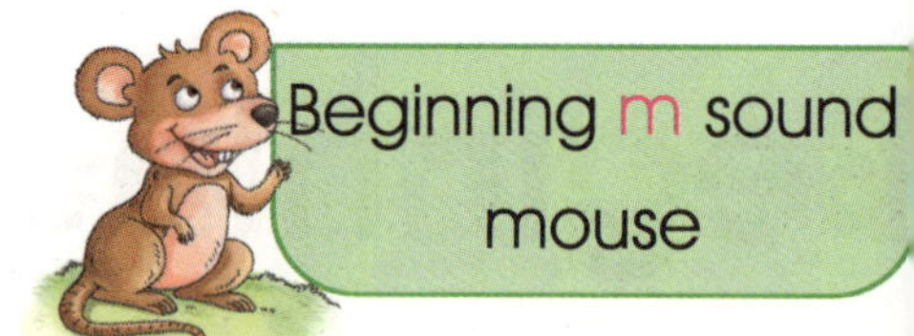

Draw a line from m to each picture whose name begins with m.

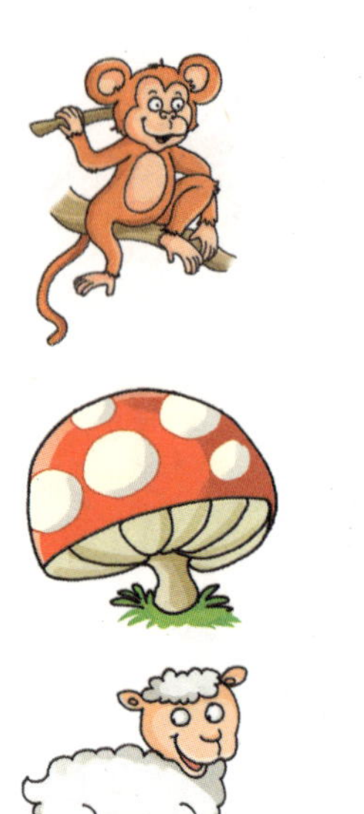

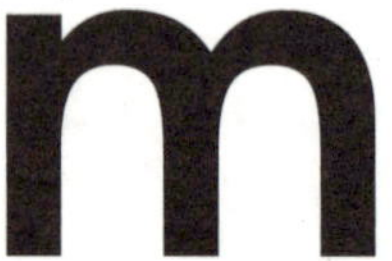

m

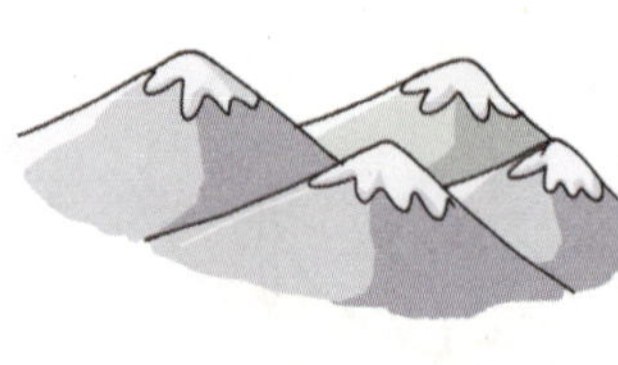

Ending m

Ending m sound
ice cream

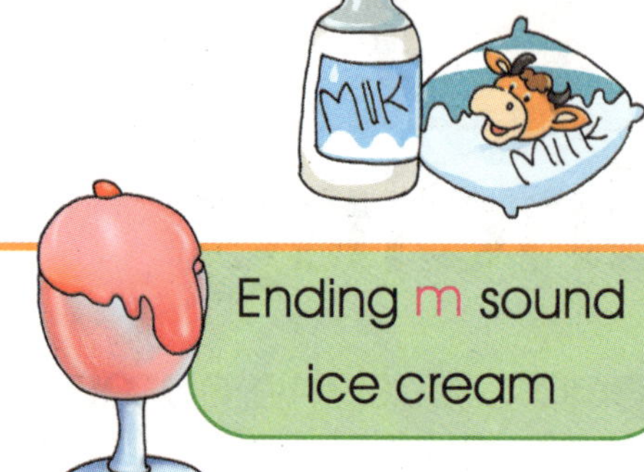

Tic-Tac-Toe

Draw a line through the pictures whose names end in m.

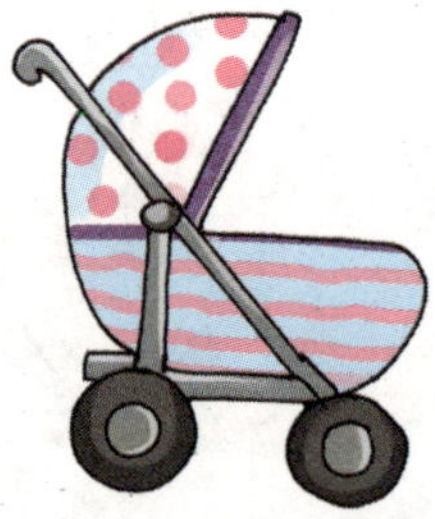

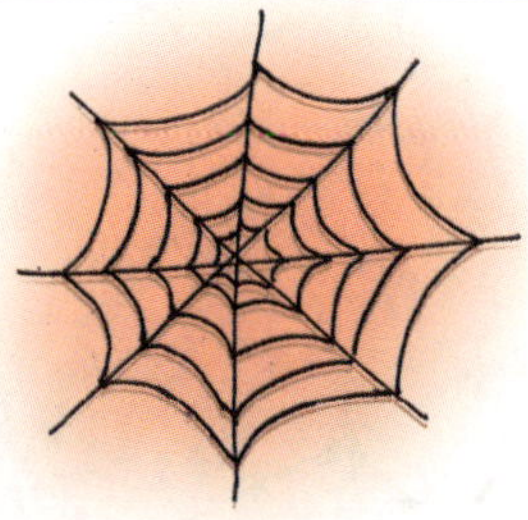

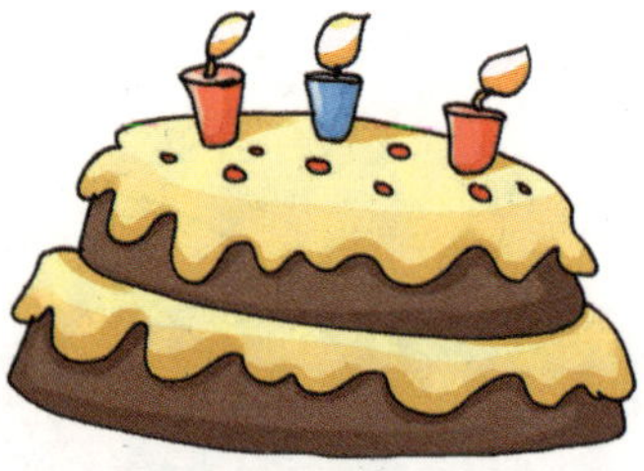

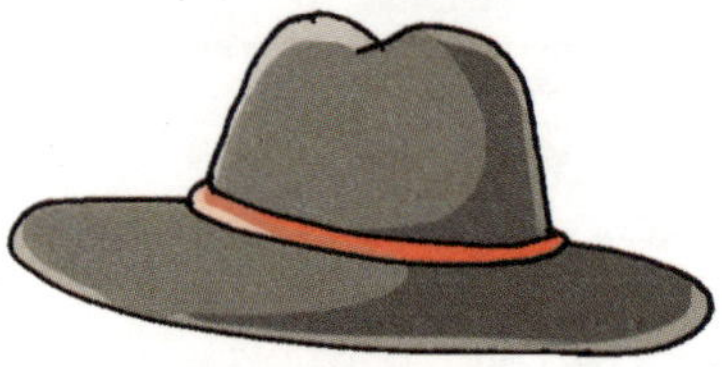

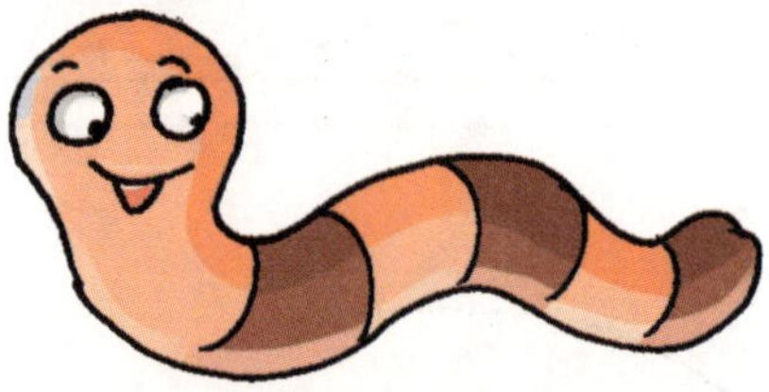

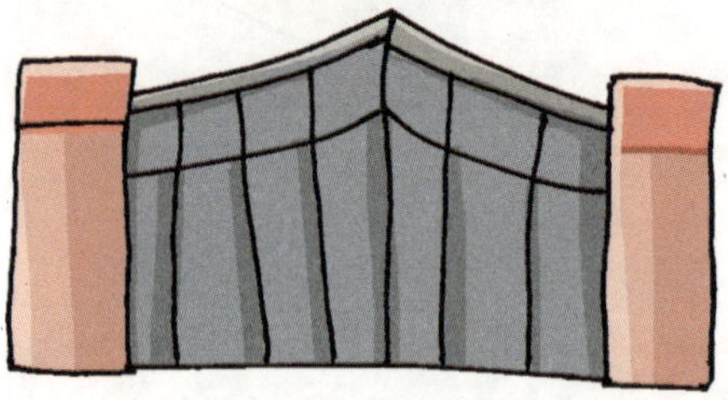

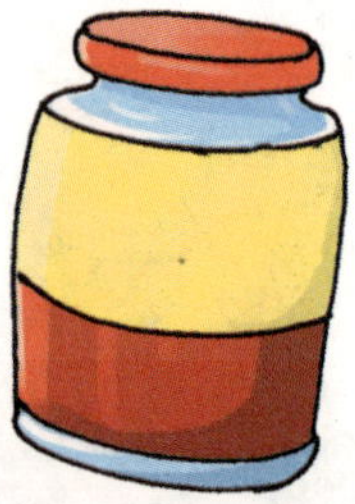

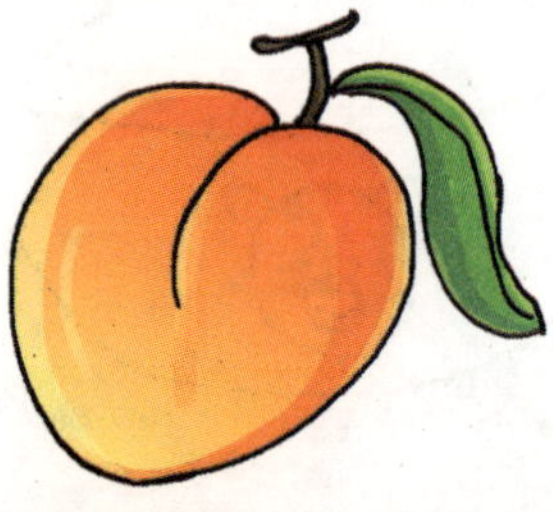

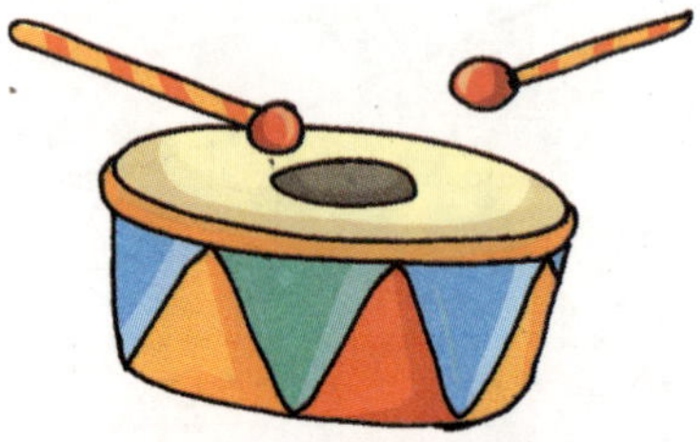

Beginning n

Write n for the pictures whose names begin with n.

   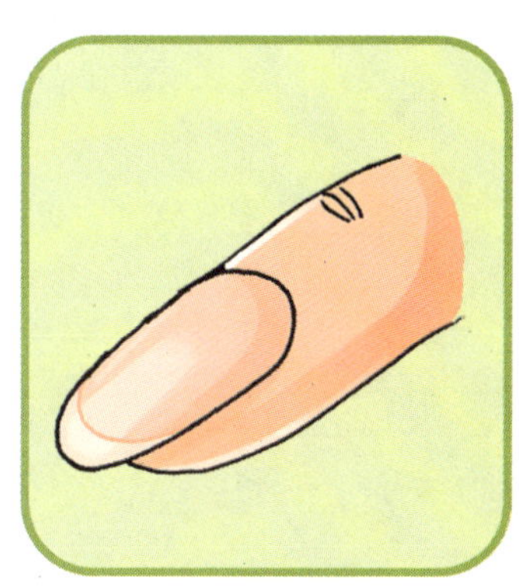

Ending n

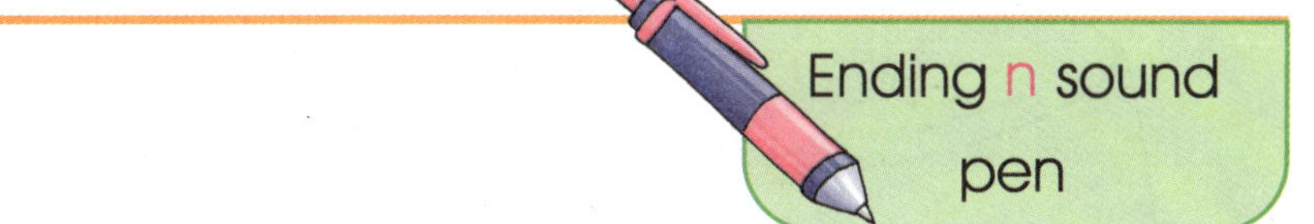

Draw a line from the words that end in letter n to n.

Beginning o

Find pictures whose names begin with the letter o. Circle (O) them.

Write o for pictures whose names begin with o.

Beginning p

Tick (✓) the pictures the names of which begin with p.

Ending p

Write p to complete the words that end with p.

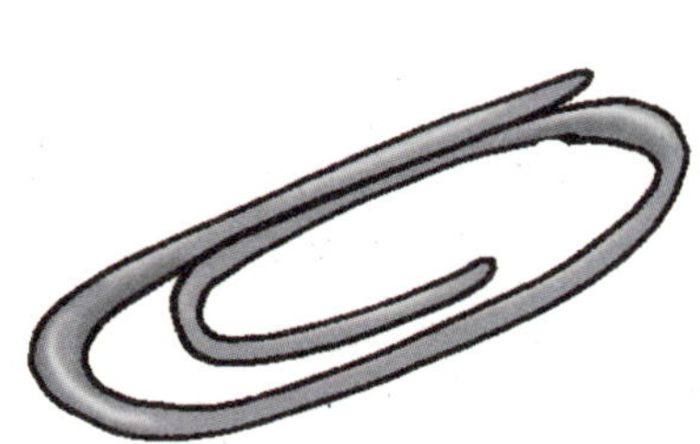

c l i

s h e e

s o a

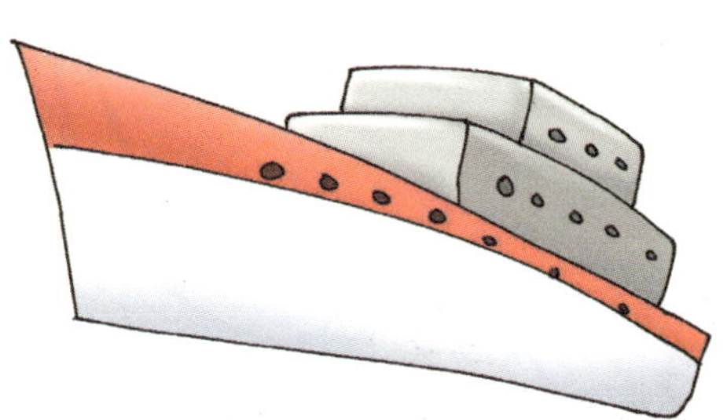

s h i

c a

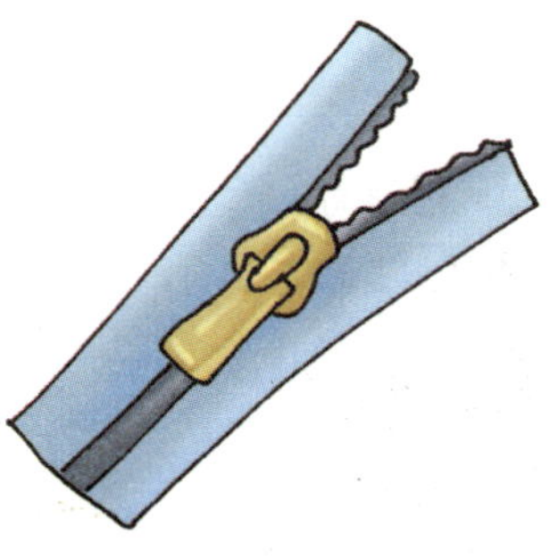

z i

Beginning q

Help the quail reach her home by following the pictures whose names begin with q.

Beginning r

Draw a circle (O) around the pictures whose names begin with r.

Ending r

Match each word to the picture whose name ends with letter r.

Beginning s

Circle (O) the pictures whose names begin with s.

Ending s

Draw lines from the pictures whose names end with s to the letter s.

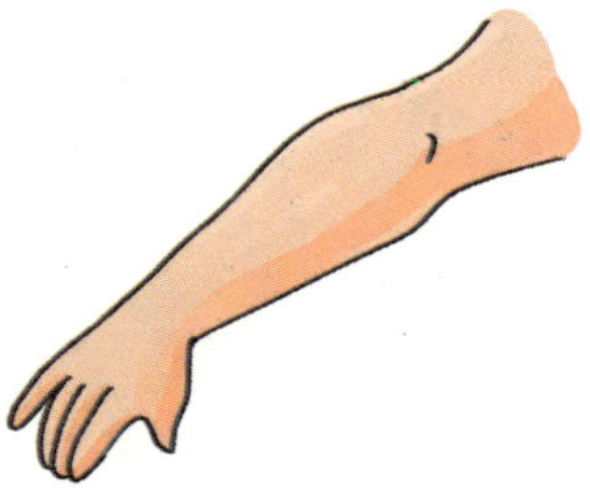

Beginning t

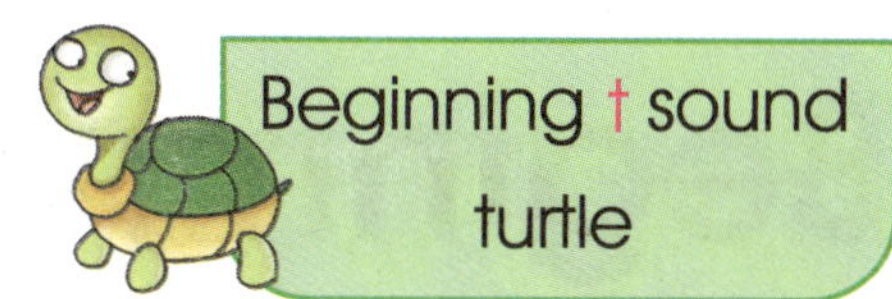

Circle (O) the pictures whose names begin with t.

Ending t

Write letter t to complete the words that end with t.

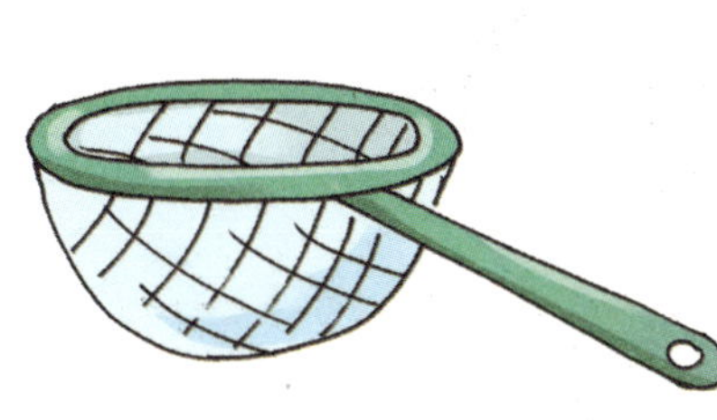

ne

ca

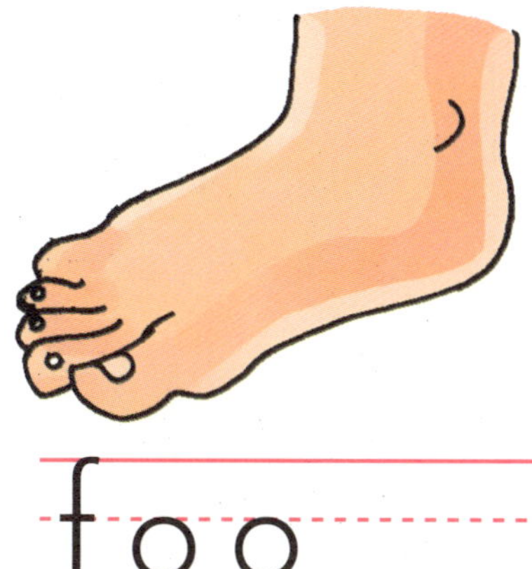

foo

boa

ma

bel

Beginning u

Beginning u sound
urn

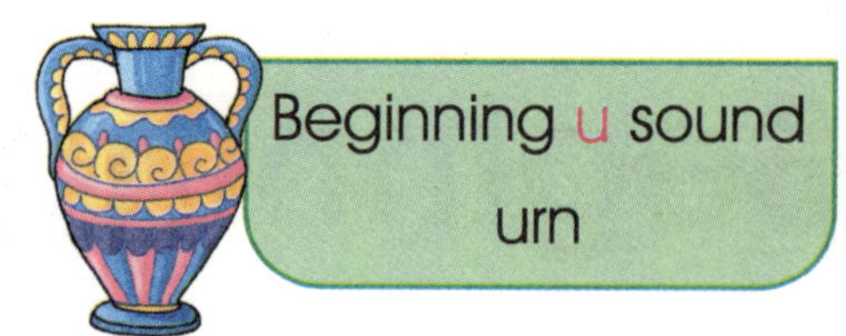

Circle (O) the pictures that begin with u.

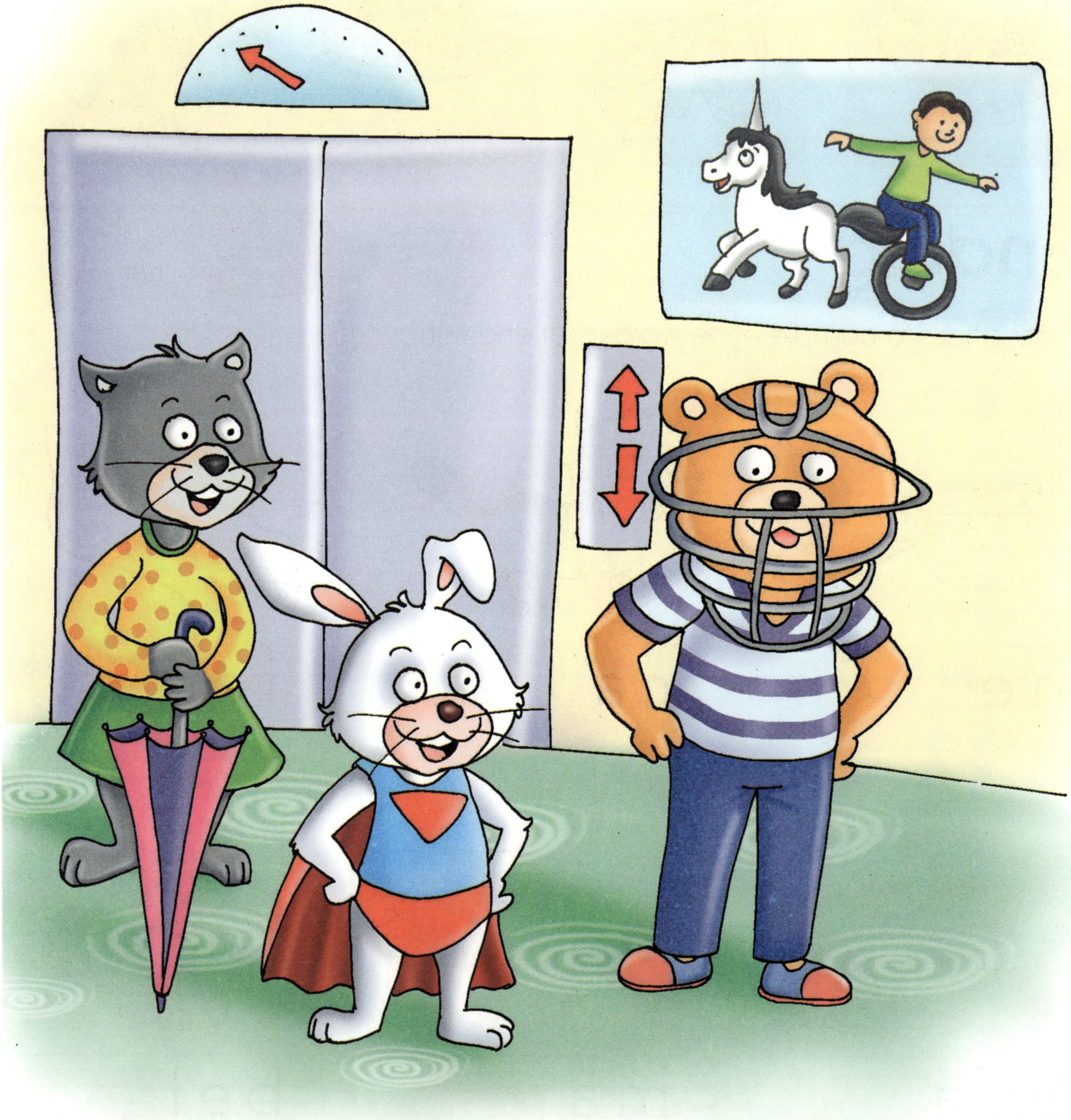

Beginning v

Circle (O) the name of each picture whose name begins with v.

Draw a line through the pictures the names of which begin with letter v.

Beginning w

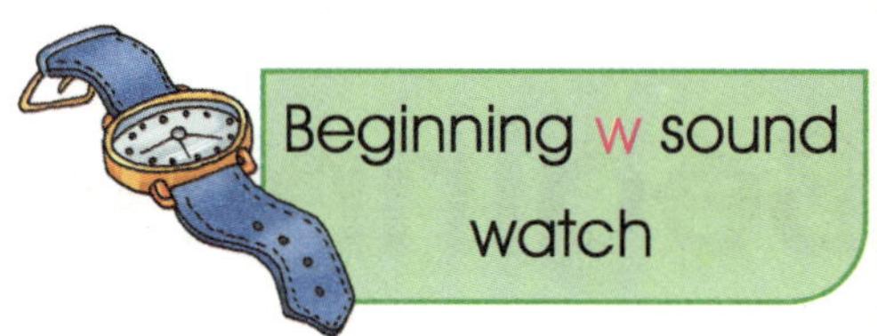

Circle (O) the pictures the names of which begin with W.

Write w for pictures whose names begin with w.

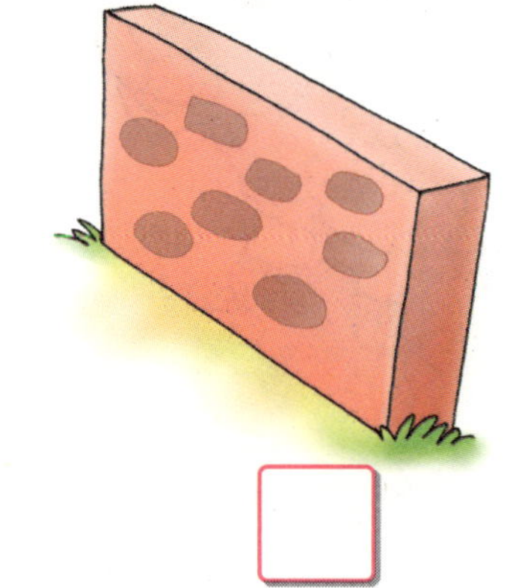

Beginning x

Tick (✓) the pictures whose names begin with x.

Ending x

Write x to complete the words that end in x.

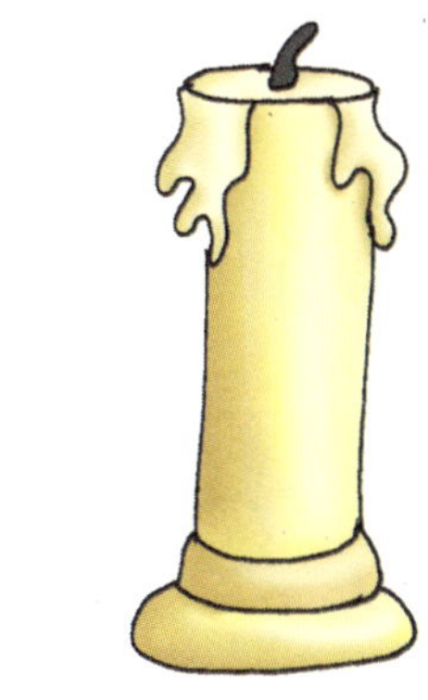

wa

fo

bo

si

Beginning y

Circle (O) the pictures whose names begin with y.

Match the word to the correct picture given below for letter y.

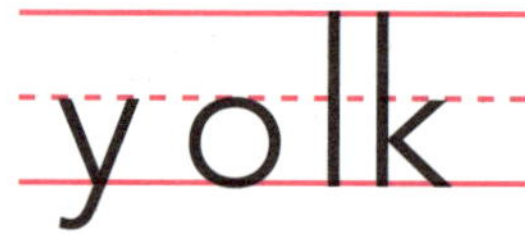

yarn

Beginning z

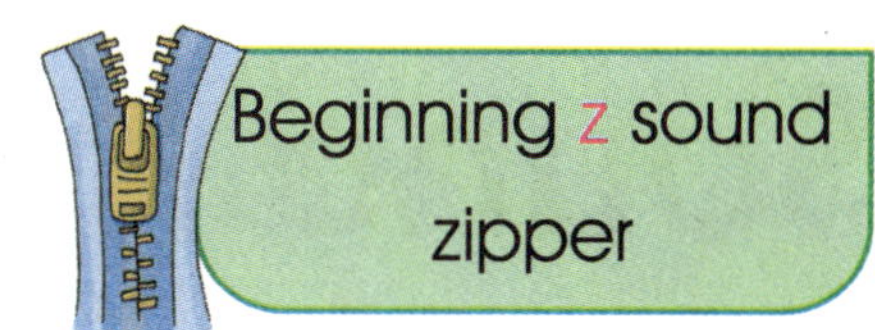

Write z for the pictures the names of which begin with z.

Draw lines from the pictures whose names begin with z to the letter z.

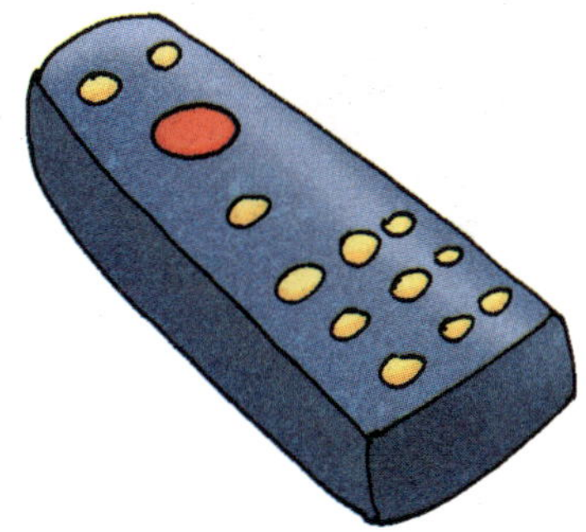

Sound It Out

Say the name of each picture. Listen to the beginning sound. Two words may have the same beginning sound in each row. Can you find them?

Missing Letters

Say the name of each picture. Write the letter that will complete the word.

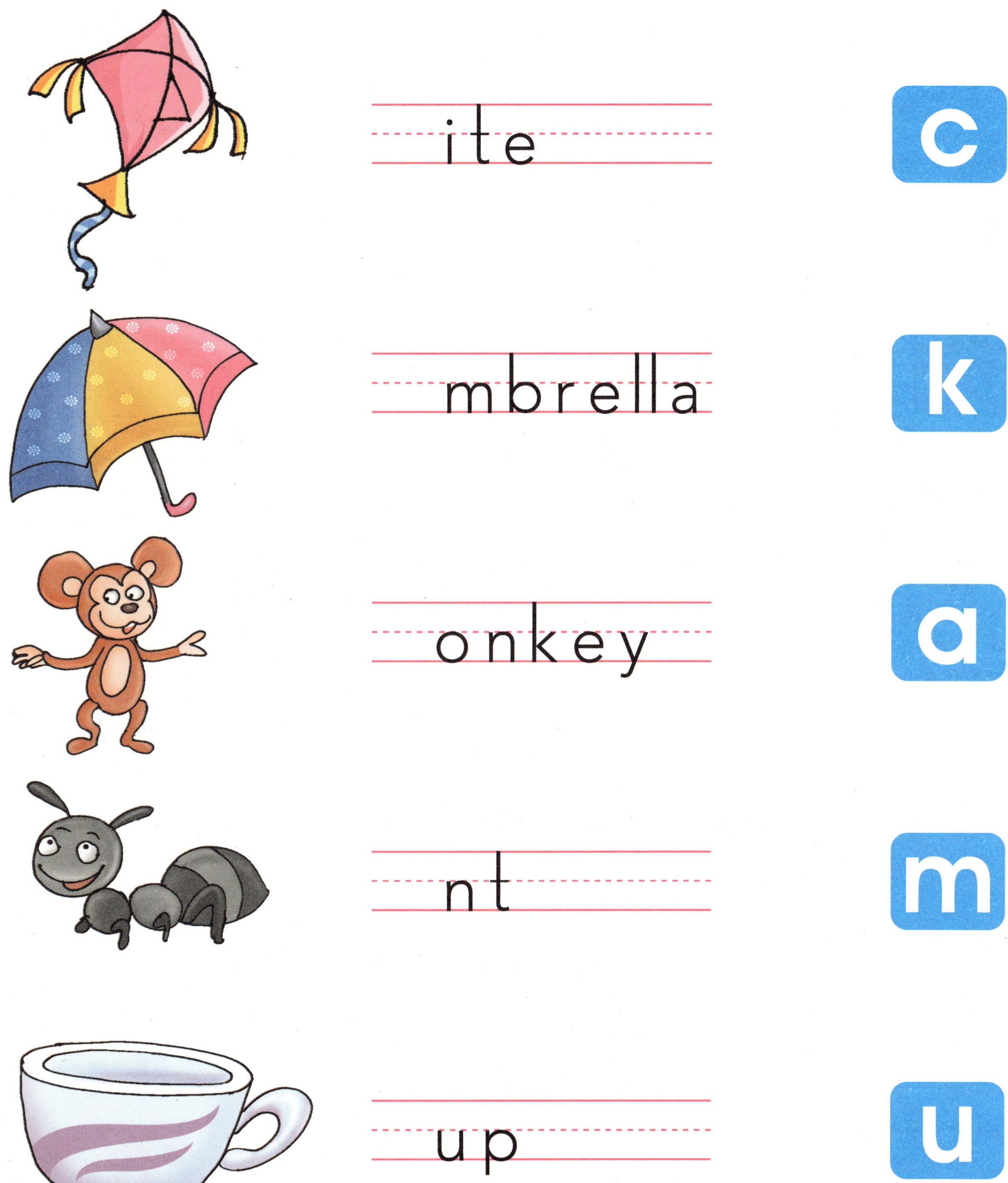

Answer Key

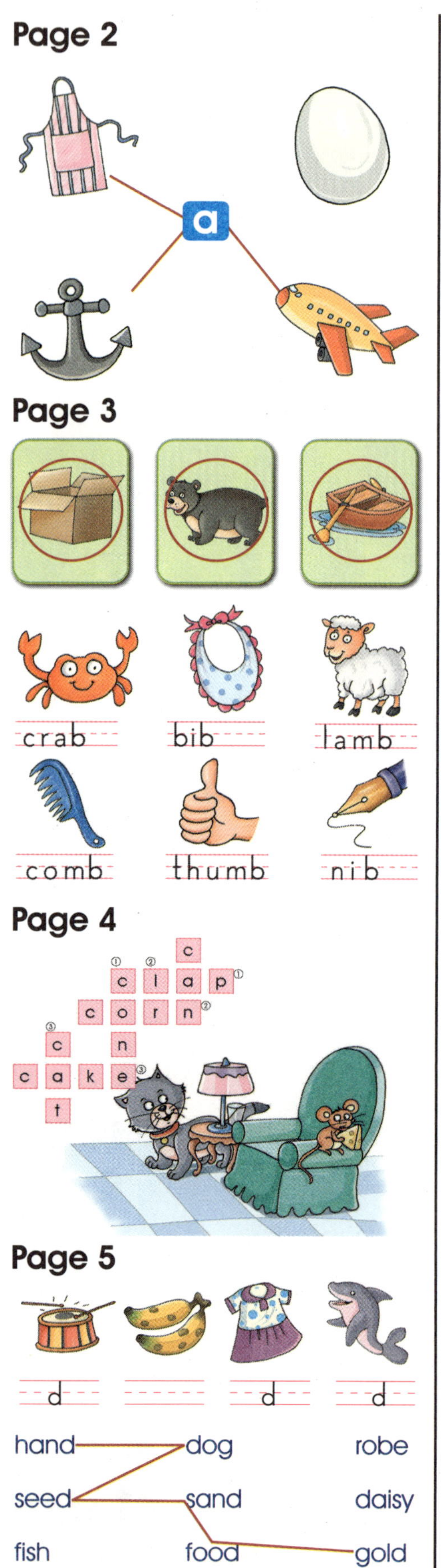
Page 2
a
Page 3
crab
bib
lamb
comb
thumb
nib
Page 4
c
c l a p
c o r n
c
n
c a k e
t
Page 5
d
d
d
hand
dog
robe
seed
sand
daisy
fish
food
gold

Page 6
Page 7
f
leaf
half
loaf
wolf
chef
roof
Page 8
log
mug
girl
ring

Page 9
h
h
h
h
h
h
h
Page 10
X
X
i
X
i
X
X
X
X
i
Page 11
j
j
j
j

Answer Key

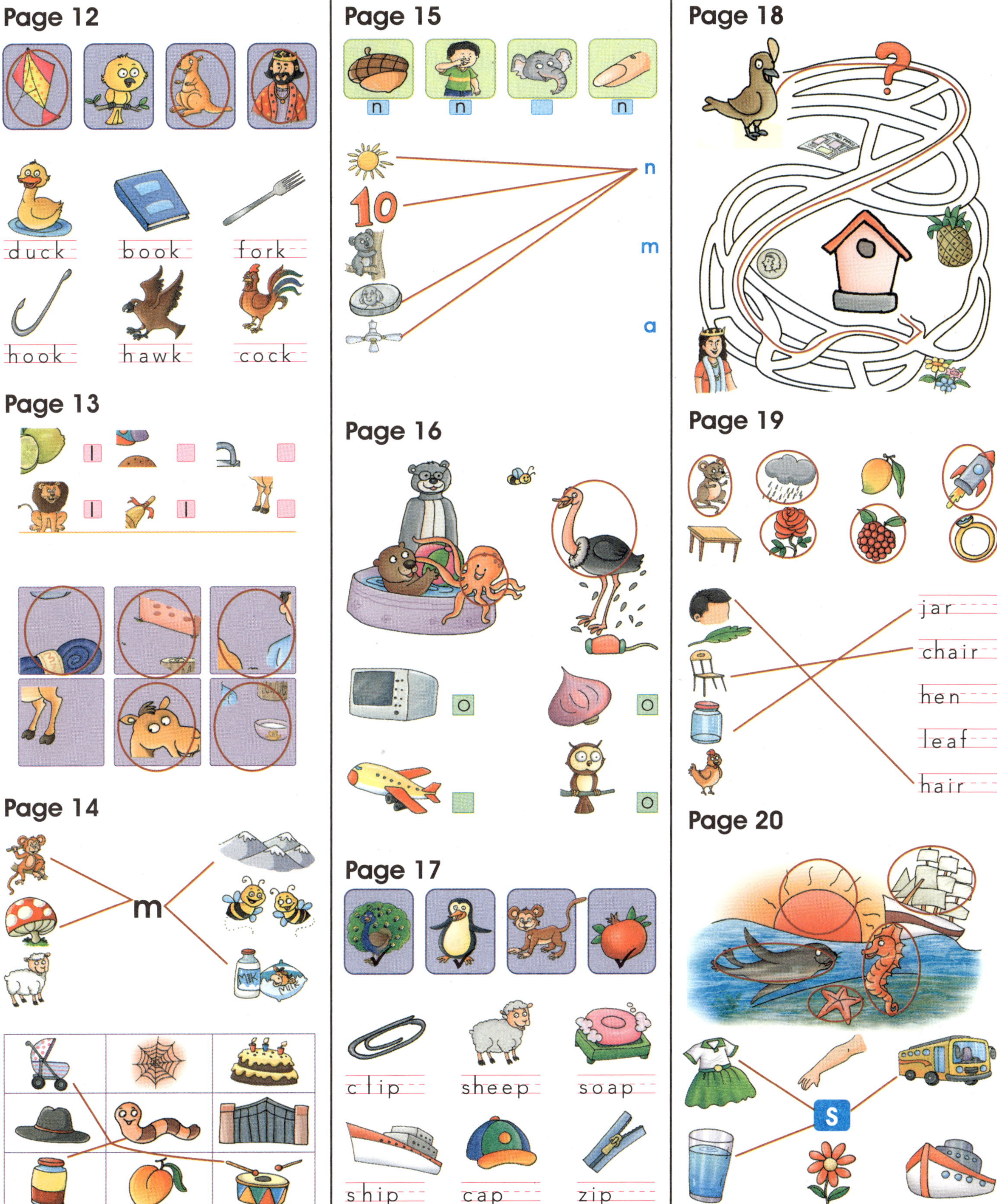

Page 12
duck
book
fork
hook
hawk
cock
Page 13
Page 14
m
Page 15
n
n
n
n
m
a
Page 16
o
o
o
Page 17
clip
sheep
soap
ship
cap
zip
Page 18
Page 19
jar
chair
hen
leaf
hair
Page 20
s

Answer Key

Page 21

Page 22

Page 23

Page 24

Page 25

Page 26

Page 27

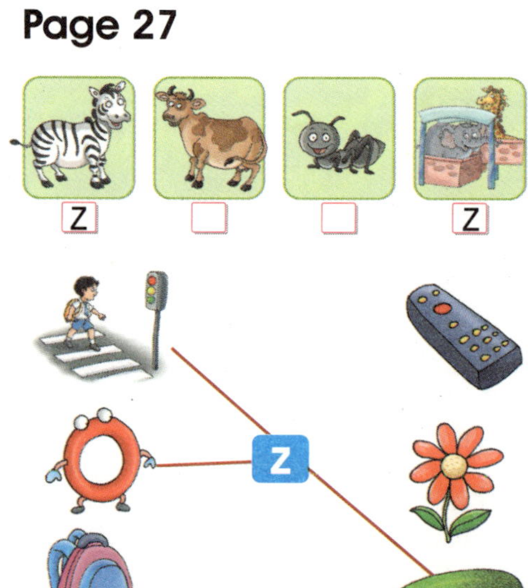

Page 29